Female Muaythai Fighters

A Brief History of Muaythai and Its People

by

Paul Metayo, PhD

Contents

Acknowledgment

This book will describe and include a brief history of Muaythai and people who practice it, a short biography of the author and a note of thanking the author's female students who have trained and fought in Boxing, Muaythai, Mixed Martial Arts and Wrestling events. The two female students whom this book included are Shauny McVeigh and Samantha Utter. These two women are competing in Boxing, Muaythai, Mixed Martial Arts, and Wrestling. The readers will see the descriptive details and pictures of Muaythai techniques which are demonstrated by Samantha and Shauny.

Part I

A brief history of Muaythai and people who practice it

1.1 The author

Paul Metayo AKA Pon in Thai started practicing Muaythai/Muay Boran at the age of 7 in Thailand with Kru Bousee, Kru Chantha, and Kru Dej. He has trained and promoted to be a Muaythai Kru in Muaythai Academy of America Association Kru program under the instruction of Kru Puk in 1991. Paul has a professional record in Thai boxing 93-11, amateur Western Boxing 11-0, professional full-contact Karate and Kickboxing 10-5. The total fighting record of 114-16.

From 1976 to 1979, while living in Pennsylvania, Paul has studied Yoga, Taichi, and Shotokan Karate, which were taught by his foster parent. From 1991 to 1993, Paul was granted three different award certificates to prepare three different martial art disciplines: Muaythai, Seido Kai Kan Karate and Boxing by the Muaythai of America Association, US Seido Kai Kan Karate Federation, and Western Regional Boxing Organization. From 1994 to 1996, Paul's gym was recognized and become a member of the World Muaythai Council Committees/World Muaythai Association, and the US Muaythai Association through the coordination of the US representative, Ajarn Tong Tiara, and the acceptance of the WMCC/WMA's chairperson, Stefan Fox

From 1996 to 2006, Paul was a president of the National Muaythai Promotion, LLC in Fresno, California under the direction and financial support of the Board of Supervisors of Dr. Toulu Thao, Gus Reyes, and Lissette Luna. From 2007 to 2013, Paul was the owner of Arizona Muaythai Academy, which is a member of Metayo Muaythai Team in Phoenix, Arizona. One reason that Paul wanted to promote Muaythai events because he has found that many non-Muaythai promoters did not provide Muaythai fighters with correct rules and regulations at their Kickboxing events.

During that time Paul had created six champions, including Alexander Gong who owned two Fairtex Muaythai gyms in San Francisco and Daly City from1995-2002 before he was shot and killed on August 2002 in the street of San Francisco, half block from his Fairtex Muaythai gym. Nevertheless, Paul's primary goal is to create new champions, provide street-effective self-defense, and top physical conditioning for persons of all fitness levels who are practicing Muaythai.

Besides operating a Muaythai school from 1991 to 2013 in California and Arizona. Paul worked for Fresno County, Health and Human Services Agency from 1985 to 2006 as a Senior Eligibility Staff, a community guest speaker for the agency to conduct and attend community conferences where he studied the culture, social-economic/political protocols. His function aimed to solve problems, pursue better opportunity and improve agency programs and services. Paul also served as a coordinator to plan and provide cultural awareness training for the county employees from 1987 to 2006. Further, Paul has worked briefly for Mendocino County, Health and Human Services Agency from1/2014 to 11/2014 as an Eligibility Supervisor. Paul has helped the agency implementing the individual caseload, individual unit, which is supervised by a supervisor, and provide training of leadership skills, human relation skill, and communication skills to both managers and staff. Paul is the 2nd Muaythai Thai trainer who went back to school and received a doctoral degree in Business Administration.

Further, Paul has published three books and a Muaythai DVD: "Mastering Muaythai with Paul Metayo", "Manual of Muaythai Techniques", "Interview with Colonel Khambou"/The Lao Resistant Force after the fall of Vietnam War, and Comparison Life in North America and Southeast Asia."

Paul Metayo

1.2 Female Muaythai Fighters

Today female Muaythai fighters are prevailing the ring in North America, Asia, Europe, Latin America, and Oceania. Many fought in amateur or professional bouts. The author has trained or helped training some of them with other trainers such as Naveen Contreras (California State/ISKA champion), Jamie Droeske (North-America champion), Lissette Pelayo, Samantha Utter, and O'Shaughnessy McVeigh. In contrast, many good female Muaythai fighters are unbeaten in Muaythai professional fighting career around the world. Since 1990, people may have seen Roxy Richardson, Marian Nakamoto, Christine Toledo, Lynda Loyce and many female Muaythai fighters who represented the US fighting in the US and abroad. Also, many good non-US female fighters are fighting in the US and around the world such as Caley Reece (Australia), Julie Kitchen (UK), Lucia Rijker (She used to represent Holland, but currently lives in the US) and many other female fighters.

Further, according to the blogs of Sylvie Von Duuglas-Ittu/ Petchrungruang (2014) who lived and fought in Thailand for a long time, stated that she was ranked number 11 among 28 female fighters and she won over 10 of them. She wrote in her blogs that Loma Lookboonmee, AKA Kanda Por Muangphet was ranked number 1 of many female fighters in Thailand. She also listed many good fighters in blogs such as Phet Jee Jaa O Meekhun, Cherry Gor Twin Gym, Saya Ito, Silvia La Notte, and Marcela Soto.

In 1913, the Thai Boxing Authority Commission in Thailand changed the Muaythai competition rules to require fighters using hand wrap, boxing gloves, and fighting in a boxing ring. Three judges would judge the fight and a referee who controls the match in the ring. The new regulation was adopted from the English boxing rules. At this time, no Thai boxing gyms in Thailand trained female fighters. According to historians and researchers, some factors influence the boxing trainers chose not to train female fighters in the past. First, based on Thai custom, the Thais have a mythical belief that if female fighters going into the boxing ring, they must crawl under the ropes, but if they jump over the lines as the male fighters did, they feared that the ring would not be sacred place for fighting anymore and could bring a bad luck to fighters. Second, the Thais believed that fighters and soldiers for the king must be male who is mentally and physically stronger than females to protect the nation against enemies. Third, the Thai males would consider that females were weaker and inferior to males, and they should respect and follow the leadership of men (Tawin, 1977)

In contrast, in 1826, King Anouvong, a king of Lanxang (Current Laos) tried to take back the Isan region where was part of Lanxang before 1779 but was invaded, destroyed, and looted by Siam (Current Thailand). Siam took the Emerald Buddha, golden Pra bang Buddha, and several important Buddha images to the Thonburi Kingdom(Current Siam/Thailand) under the administration of King Taksin. According to Thai history, when King Anouvong army arrived in the City of Korat where Yai Mai Mo, or "Grandma Mo" who was the deputy governor's wife recruited women in the city to kill the Lao soldiers with the kitchen knives during the time they rested and slept. Because of her action, King Taksin of Siam has credited and recognized her as a heroine of the country. The king gave her a new name "Thao Suranari to honor her as a brave woman with a man name because the word "Thao" means "mister" in English, and the word "Thao" used to address a man in Thai and Lao custom. Therefore, history has been written and proven that women are not weaker or inferior to men when opportunities are given and not rejected (Supalak & Potkin, 2006)

Nonetheless, in the mid-1990s, many female martial artists from New Zealand, Australia, the US, and European countries started going to Thailand to train in Muaythai, and many are fighting in Muaythai events. Today, you can see female Muaythai fights events in every continent, Asia, Europe, Africa, the US, and Oceania.

For this reason, Thai Muaythai trainers started training female fighters to compete with female foreigners. Many Thais have experienced that women can put up with pain and maintain the disciplines of the sport better than men. Of course, male fighters still dominate the games, but women have proven that they are also as competitive as men are in martial competition and other cases of life. Training in Muaythai requires effort, time, dedication, patience, and determination.

Today, we can find many female Muaythai fighters match by watching Youtube, Pay-per-View, or going to the fight events such as Legend Kickboxing, Glory Kickboxing, Women fight, National Muaythai Promotion, and other Muaythai events through the US and the world. As a result, many studies reported that Muaythai training promotes a healthy lifestyle, active and energetic. Muaythai training helps cut weight, change diet, feel though, gain a healthy life, have fun, excite mentally and physically through self-confidence and truthfulness of oneself (Nguyen, 2018).

Below are some Muaythai Techniques which are demonstrated by Samantha and Shauny.

Shauny Teeb to counter Samantha's right straight punch

Shauny Kicks Samantha's standing leg to counter the high kick to the head

After blocking the left hook from Samantha, Shauny follows up with back Elbow

After blocking Samantha's right straight punch, Shauny counters it with right knee

After parrying Samantha's left jab, Shauny counters it with back elbow

After blocking Samantha's right straight punch, Shauny counters it with right knee

After blocking Samantha's left hook, Shauny counters it with left knee

After parrying Samantha's right straight punch, Shauny counters it with right straight punch

After blocking Samantha's right hook, Shauny counters it with right up elbow

A picture of Shauny throwing a left kick during her Amateur Muaythai fight [We can't show her opponent in the book]

Shauny thumbs up after winning a Muaythai fight

1.3 Who are Thais and where did they come from?

Nan Zhao Territory

In the past, Muaythai/Thai boxing, = (Toy, or Tee Muay) is a combat sport of Tai Kadai people (Lao and Thai), which was recorded by the Chinese in Yunnan province between the years 700s-1100s CE before these people moved southward to new lands (Sor Sae Li, 1982). The writers did not report when Muaythai was initially invented but stated it is a dangerous and sophisticated martial art discipline, and the Tai Kadai who practiced it was very good at it. From the 8th century to the 19th century, the Thai Siam, Thai-Lao and Khmer have been initially practicing it. Today, with the globalization, Muaythai is practicing worldwide by all martial art discipline practitioners. By 700, the Tai Kadai started writing their history, and Muaythai was included in it. The last Tai Kadai's kingdom was Nanchao, or Nan Zhao (750s CE), where King Khunburom was the head of the state and has defeated the invasions and expansion of the Chinese and Mongol who were led by Ku Blai Khan (grandson of Genghis Khan) four times, but Nanchao/Nan Zhao was finally defeated and seized by the Mongol in 1253 (Sasombat 1990).

Khmer Empire

From 700s to 1200s CE, the Khmer Empire (Cambodia) has expanded its territory from Angkor Wat area to north and north-west region of the Indochina (Cambodia, Laos, and Vietnam). In consequence, 100 thousand of Ta Kadai have left Nanchao and moved southward to settle in the Khmer Empire as refugees and considered the region as their new home. If you look at the white line on the map below, you will see that the white line is the Mekong River that passes through both sides of Laos or used to be called Lanxang (3rd Tai Kadai family's kingdom) in the 16th century. You can read about the French helped create Laos and get out from the control of Siam in 1853, and the French officially colonized it in 1893 (Fortini, 1973). The map below shows the Khmer Empire before Siam, Lanna, and Lanxang were found.

Siam/Sukhothai/Ayutthaya

In 1248 while the Khmer Empire's power was shatteringly falling, the Thai-Siam took over the land and declared their first independence state: "Sukhothai". Also, the Thai-Siam kept pushing the Khmer southward from one city to another such as Ayutthaya, Thonburi on Maenam Chao Praya (River), and finally establish Bangkok (Krung Thep in Thai) as their new capital city on the Gulf of Siam. The Kingdom of Ayutthaya (Old capital city of Siam, which was taken from the Khmer Empire) in the 16th century. The map also indicates Kingdom of Lanna, established in 1259 (2nd Kingdom of Tai Kadai, but joined Thailand in 1775 to avoid the English control, and in 1776, Siam took control of Lanna, and finally annexed it into Thailand in 1920), Kingdom of Lan Xang (Laos), and The Shrinking Khmer Empire (Cambodia). The Thai-Lao also established their independent state as Lanxang in 1353, Luang Prabang was the capital city at that time. Lanxang was the land situated on **both sides of Mekong River** at that time too (see the map below). [Laos was called Lanxang before the French colonization], and Thailand was called Siam before 1948, 1949 and 1950. When King Khunburom ordered his two sons to move southward and find new lands. The first son led the Tai-Siam group, and the second son led the Tai-Lao group, and they conquered two different territories [keep reading the story, and you will understand the history] (Khambou, 1989)

Below is the map of Laos(Lanxang), Lanna, Ayudhya-Siam, Cambodia-(Khmer), Champa, and Dai Viet in the 13th century.

The word "Siam" means Dark or Thief in the Khmer language because the Thais came from Current China and Settled with the Khmer Empire as refugees and then took the opportunity to make the land when Khmer Empire power was weakening. However, the Khmer have help prince Fa-Ngum unite Lanxang Land and become a king. Fa-Ngum grew up in the Khmer Empire before he came up with 6000 Khmer soldiers to unite separate dynasties into one Lanxang. Lanxang territories were Muang PhaiNam, Muang Sua, and Muang Champasak before 1353 CE. (Le Boise, 1970)

Muaythai VS Japanese Judo & Karate

However, Muaythai became the national sport of Thailand in 1913, and people in Laos called it Muay-Lao, and the Khmer called it Muay-Khmer. By the late 1960s, the Japanese-Karate-dos have fought against Muaythai three consecutive years and lost all three times. They decided to hire former Thai boxers to train them after those events. In consequence, they have incorporated some Muaythai techniques into many of their new Karate styles.

Based on this interest, the Japanese martial artists have invented Japan Kickboxing and other European and American martial artists who mostly practiced Japanese martial arts have also developed American Kickboxing and International Kickboxing. Nevertheless, Muaythai has been recognized and accepted to practice by both civilian and military groups worldwide. As we can see that Mixed Martial Artists use Muaythai in their competitions such as UFC, Sansou, K-1 Kickboxing, Glory Kickboxing, Legend Kickboxing and many other MMA events (Metayo & Keo, 1990)

Siam and Lanxang War

In 1779. Lanxang (Laos), was divided into three independent states: Luang Prabang in the North, Vientiane in the Central, where included the Korat Plateau, which is now part of new Thailand's provinces and Champasak in the South. At the same time, General Thaksin, (who later became King of Thailand, and was recognized as Rama I of Thonburi Dynasty). Had driven the Burmese from Siam, and took advantage of Lanxang chaos; Thus, overrun all three dynasties' of Lanxang. He ordered to move all Lao royal family's members to the west side of the Mekong River in Isan area to prevent the Lao regroup and rebellion. He also took many of Lao Royal family's members as prisoners. Thaksin took the Emerald Buddha and Phra Bang images from Vientiane (Phra Bang and Emerald Buddha are the sacred statues that are worshiped by Lao people, they are represented as the image of Buddha, and were placed in Vientiane, which is the capital of Lanxang, and Lao people celebrate these images with a large and week-long ceremony annually). For the readers to understand the history, the author pointed out that Siam has four dynasties from 1248-present: Sukhothai, Ayudhya, Thonburi, and Bangkok. (Bangkok is called Krungthep in Thai); Siam changed its country name to Thailand in 1948 by General Plaek Phi bun Song Kham. The general later became a prime minister of Thailand (To legitimize the country to include all Thai people. Therefore, he changed the country name from Siam to Thailand, and because General Plaek Phi bun Song Kham had an education from France, and inspired Hitler's philosophy; therefore, he governed Thailand with the dictatorship ideology).

Lanxang (Laos)

Laos lost the battle to Siam and was under its suzerainty from 1779 to 1893. Among 16 provinces that Lanxang (Laos) lost to Siam (Thailand) at that time, Korat Plateau was the first province that Siam recognized, administered, and assimilated as part of Siam (the readers can read about this reason later in the book). Lao people including their royal family's members were recruited to do hard labor (corvee labor), digging waterway canals around Bangkok (these canals are covered up now to conceal the hardship, suffering and harsh punishment of Lao people in the past), and several hard/unpaid labors, beaten until death. The Suzerainty in Asia in the past is to secure the population centers for corvee labor, regional control trade, and confirm religious and secular by the controlling country, but allowing the sovereign authority in its internal affairs with the controlling supervision and officials' selection by the dominant country (Pavi, 1966)

Toward the end of 1826, one Lao prince (Anouvong) who was released from Bangkok and was authorized to be a king in Vientiane, Lanxang (Laos) plotted a rebellion against Siam. His army started to capture several Isan provinces, including Korat Plateau (Nakhon Ratchasima part of new Thailand) and reached Saraburi. At this point, Lao people who lived in the right bank of the Mekong River started moving north, so this caused the advance of Anouvong army. Anouvong army lost this battle against Siam for three reasons: one the flood of Lao refugees from Saraburi pushing north slowed down his army, another was the disruption of Yai Mae Mo's young women who tried to seduce and drunk Anouvong soldiers. She tried to help Siam's army instead of liberating Lao suzerainty from Siam. Third, the English gave Siam a large arms stockpile of Napoleonic Wars in Europe. The English under the Burney Treaty signed in Bangkok on 20 June 1826 between Henry Burney, an agent of British East India Company, and King Rama III of Siam to recruit Siam as an ally of Britain to fight Burma (Burma was called the Kingdom of Eva at that time) (Surichai, 1976).

This brief history tells the readers that even though Thai Siam, Thai Lao, and Thai Lanna came from the same father, Khun Borom from Nanchao (Yunnan province in Modern China), they fought each other poorly with bitter revenge, punishment, and prejudice. This history will tell the readers that Muaythai does not belong to only Thailand even though it is developed and recognized by the Thai State Athletic Commission. People in Lanna (Chiangmai, Chiang Rai, cities in current/northern Thailand), and Laos practice Muaythai too, but it is not developed and supported by their government. The French who colonized Laos from 1893 to 1954 introduced new sports for Lao people to practice, especially soccer. The

French fought a war with Siam in 1941 to claim Champasak and Sayaburi for Laos from the Isan region (Isan means Northeast region of Thailand) where is on the west bank of the Mekong River that Laos lost to Thailand in 1779 (Sor Sae Li, 1982)

Muaythai/Muay Boran

Muaythai became worldwide in the 20th century because it defeated notable practitioners of other martial arts. The readers can read an article, written by Hardy Stockman in 1990 "Muaythai versus the Rest" One verse said that Muaythai fighters do not brag how good they are, but stay humble, and show their talent in the ring, and let the audience be the judges. The Professional Boxing Association of Thailand governs the professional league of Muaythai fighters, and most events are sanctioned by the Sports Authority of Thailand, and the World Muaythai Federation oversees and collaborates the Muaythai events around the globe where Muaythai event is taking place with other organizations.

Muaythai practitioners call Muaythai the "Art of Eight Limbs" or the "Science of Eight Limbs" because they are using two (2) hands, two (2) elbows, two (2) knees and two (2) feet, and these human body's components are equal to eight (8) weapons to be used by Nak Muay, the Practitioner of Muaythai, or Muaythai fighter. The Thai would call White European Muaythai Practitioners: "Nak Muaythai Farang."

The word "Farang."

The word “Farang” comes from the mispronunciation of Thai people who when they first met the French even though the French were not the 1st westerner came to Thailand, but the Dutch did. However, the French had a significant and influential political role, as a minister-level in the kingdom during the Ayudhya period in the 16th century.

Anyway, the Thai had a lousy time trying to pronounce the word “Francaise” when they had to refer these white people from abroad to their friends. Their ears were not familiar with this strange accent. The word referring to them gradually changed to Farang, and it has been used since then to refer all Caucasians with white skin from abroad. During the Vietnam War, 1955-1975, many Black American soldiers from the US stationed in Thailand with White American soldiers; thus, they called these individuals "Farang Dum". Dum means black in Thai. Thai has a hard time to pronounce other languages, especially, European Languages even though they like to speak them. If they can use a word of English for example, they would be proud to speak it even though they pronounce it incorrectly. For example, the Thai would pronounce the word "Apple" = "Appearn", because they simply say the word, but not completely pronounce it as the Native-born English speakers do. We would rarely see Thai officials, journalists, faculties or students who can fluently speak foreign languages even though they study those languages at the levels. However, in 2014, the first Thai female prime minister who has education in the US, speaks English well, so that she often corresponded with foreign news Media. The former US president, Barak Obama has met her in Thailand (Richardson, 2014). The pictures below are a complimentary to the author by Bob Richardson who visited Thailand in 2014. He collected the story and pictures from a Thai Newspaper (Thairath, 2014). According to his research, Bob said that he found three Thai prime ministers who had an education in the US and speak English well. The first one was Dr. Taksin Shinawatra who was the prime minister of Thailand of two terms from 02/09/2001-09/19/2006. The second prime minister was Dr. Abhisit Vejjajira, 12/17/2008-08/05/2011. The third one was a Kentucky State University Graduate, Yingluck Shinawatra who was the prime minister of Thailand from 08/05/2011-05/07/2014.

When did Muay Boran change its name to Muaythai?

In 1913, the Thai Boxing Authority Commission considered calling Muay Boran [Muay-Boran has both stand-up and ground fighting] "Muaythai" by codifying the English Boxing Rules into Thai Boxing Competition. The English boxing was also introduced into the curriculum of colleges and universities in Thailand, and in 1919, Western Wrestling and Japanese Judo were also taught as sports in the curriculum of all colleges and universities in Thailand. We may see that some Muaythai fighters rarely use punches in the fight, and some of us misunderstand that they do not know Boxing and offer to help them out. The fact is they practice it and can use it very well when it is necessary to use the boxing skills in the fight.

In conclusion, the author hopes the readers understand where Muaythai comes from and how it is evolving through the history of Siam, Lanna, Lanxang, and other western countries that involved in the affairs of Siamese history such as Burma, Malaysia, France, Britain, Portugal, and Holland. The main reason that Siam changed its name to Thailand because its population is from Tai Kadai: (Thai-Lao, Thai-Lanna, Thai Malay, Thai-Khmer, and Thai-Mon). Siam represents only Sukhothai, Ayutthaya, Thonburi, and Krungthep (Bangkok). Therefore, the name "Thailand" appropriately represents all people. Thai Siamese is adventurist and wants to explore and conquer other territories. For instance, Siam invaded Angkor Wat kingdom in 1549, but was defeated, and has tried again and again several times in the past, and even in the modern time, but was conquered by the Khmer and French Armies in the past, or by the UN resolution in the contemporary time. Some people speak Khmer in three provinces in Thailand: Buriram, Surin, and Sisaket. Buakaw Banchamek (Sombat Banchamek), A top Muaythai fighter, was born and grew up in Surin where half of the city, people speak Khmer, and the other half, speak Lao/ Lao Isan. People in five southern provinces in Thailand also speak Malay: Narathiwat, Pattani, Yala, Songkhla, Satun, some population in Ranong and Phuket also speak Malay. If the readers study Thailand neighbor countries' history, they would understand that Siam had fought many wars against its neighbors and seized many territories (Thawin, 1977)

Part II

Muaythai Techniques of Metayo Muaythai Academy

General Thai Terms for Muaythai

Punch = Mat

Kick = Tae

Jab = Taae

Straight punch = Trong

Hook = Vieng

Uppercut = Soi Down

Left = Sai

Right = Kua

Roundhouse kick = Tae Vieng

Cut-Kick = Tae Tat

Back Kick or spin Back Kick = Tae Vieng Krab

Kick to the body + Tae Lum Toi

Kick to the leg = Tae Ka

Kick High = Tae Soong

Kick Low = Tae Tam

Straight Axe Kick = Tae Kat Na

Foot Jab or pushed-Kick = Teeb

Foot jab to the leg = Teeb ka

Foot jab to the body + Teeb lum toi

Foot jab to the face + Teeb Na or bat ha loob Pak

Elbow = Sok

Knee = Kao

Knee strike without clinch = Kao Loi

Knee strike with clinch = Kao Hol

Lead elbow = Sok tat

Rear Elbow = Sok Trong

Up elbow = Sok Ngat

Down Elbow = Sok Nam

Required Hours of training of Metayo Muaythai

Basic Level (1) requires 60 hours of training before students are eligible for examination

Intermediate Level (2) requires 75 hours of training before students are eligible for examination

Advance Level (3) requires 90 hours of training before students are eligible for examination

Kru Level (4) requires 125 hours of training before students are eligible for testing. Kru Level requires additional knowledge and skills. These include Muaythai Strategy, Muaythai techniques, Muaythai History, Background of the candidate in martial arts and purpose of acquiring to be a Kru (I will send this requirement to you later. I am still writing it)

Note: We may adjust the hours of training for students who have fight experience in the past by 75%-50% after we observe, analyze and evaluate their knowledge and skills for 20-24 hours (7 to 8 weeks) to see if their techniques are matching ours

Kru Level (4) after passing the test, Kru candidates will receive a copy of Muaythai Manual for teaching, including items for all levels training, all levels testing, and Thai and Muaythai history in the same book. The Kru test includes 125 hours of training, answer the questions in the Kru Request Form, and teaching evaluation from students, if all these tests are not successful, the candidate will be allowed to extend their training for 3-4 months, where the trainers will review every Muaythai techniques with him/her before granting a certificate. Level 2, 3 and Kru students should practice the Wai Kru: "Yang Sam Kum" and "Hanuman Vieng Kra-bong".

Items for Practice & Exam

Level 1 Practice

Stretch 4 minutes

Jump rope 9 minutes

Foot work

Taae, trong, vieng ngat

Sok trong, tat, ngat, krab, and nam

Kao Loi, Hol, Ra, Tee and Tank

Teeb sai, Kua, Side Kick, and Teeb Krab

Tae Vieng, Tae Sorn, Tae Tat, Tae trong, Tae vieng krab

Sit-up 50 crunches

50 Push-up

Level 2 Practice

Stretch 4 minutes

Jump rope 5 rounds

Foot work

Bang Taae with 4 different techniques

Bang Mat trong with 4 different techniques

Bang mat vieng with 4 different techniques

Avoid and Bang Mat Ngat with 4 different techniques

Bang 4 different Sock's

Bang 4 different Teeb

Bang Kao Hol, Kao Ra, and Tee

Bang Tae vieng, Tae Lang, Tae Lum-toi, Tae krab and Tae tat

60 Push-up

60 Sit up

Level 3 Practice

Stretch 4 minutes

Jump rope 7 rounds

Foot work

Taae, and defenses against it in 4 different techniques

Tae and defenses against it in 4 different techniques

Teeb and defenses against it in 4 different techniques

Kao and defenses against it in 4 different techniques

Sok and defenses against it in 4 different techniques

Mat and defenses against it in 4 different techniques

Sparring strategies 3 rounds sparring, 3 minutes each round with 1minute break

70 Push-up

70 Sit up

Techniques for All Levels Training

Stance: Hand and Foot Positions

Foot work: Move in & out; side to side

Foot Jab & Defense against Foot Jab (Teeb)

Tae & Defense against Tae

Mat Trong & Defense against Mat Trong

Kao & defense against Kao

Mat Vieng & Defense against Mat Vieng

Sok & Defense against Sok

Offensive & Defensive Techniques

Offensive	Defensive
1) Lead Foot Tae	Tae Sorn
2) Mat Trong	Teeb
3) Rear Foot Tae & Mat Trong	Kao or Teeb & Vieng & Tae
4) Lead Foot Teeb &Lead Kao	Step Aside & Tae
5) Taae & Trong & Lead Foot Tae	Back off-to-right & Tae Tat
6) Tae, Teeb & Kao Loi	Kao Block, Dun & Mat Trong
7) Taae, Taae, Teeb & Tae	Back off, De-direct, block & Lead Tae

Part III

Required Techniques to practice for Metayo Muaythai Academy System Ranking Test

Level (1) **Novice Muaythai Exam Techniques**:

Jab
Jab and cross
Jab, cross, hook
Jab, cross, hook and straight

Jab, cross, left elbow
Jab, cross, hook, right elbow

Right and left uppercut, spin back elbow

Right straight knee

Left straight knee

right and left knees alternately

Side snap knee left and right alternately

Left Teeb, right kick

right Teeb, left kick

right Teeb, left Teeb, and back leg kick, or spin back kick

Left jab, right kick

Right cross, left kick

left and right punches, left kick

jab, cross, hook, right kick

left jab, low inside left kick

left jab, low inside left kick, and middle section left kick

right punch, low inside left kick, and right kick to body

left jab, low right kick to the leg, right punch and left kick to the body

Clinch, right and left side knee, and right and left straight knee

Level (2) Intermediate Muaythai Exam Techniques

Defenses against the lead jab: block it with the right hand and counter with the lead jab; prevent it with the right hand and counter with the lead hook; step to your right and counter with the right straight punch; step back-right a little and counter with a right uppercut and lead hook

Block with right hand and counter with lead leg kick; block with right hand and counter with lead knee strike with lead hand grabbing opponent left shoulder or neck.

Block with the right hand and counter with lead up-elbow, or lead side elbow, or right elbow, or turn back elbow

Defenses against the Rear punch [right punch for right-handed fighter]: slip the punch to your left and counter with a left hook, or block the right punch and counter with a right punch

Block the right punch, and counter with a right kick, or back off a little and use left Teeb and then right kick,

Move right a little, block the right punch from inside and grab the opponent neck with the right hand and then throw right knee.

Defenses against left hook: Block the hook, grab the opponent neck and turn him or her to your left, then left knee strike, duck under the hook slightly to avoid the hook, and counter with either right from outside or left a hook to the abdomen,

Back off and counter with either right or left kick

Defenses against right kick: Raise left knee to block and counter with a left kick, follow up with punches, block with left elbow and counter with a right punch, left hook, and right kick, Teeb with the left foot and follow up with the right kick

Step in closer and push with the left hand and use left foot to sweep opponent standing leg

Defenses against Left Kick: Raise up left or right knee to block and counter with a right kick,

Block with the right elbow, and counter with the left hook, right punch, and left kick; step closer and to your forward left, and use the right kick to sweep opponent standing leg

Defenses against clinches: lock opponent right arm with a left hand, use right hand to grab the opponent neck and pull to your right and counter with right-side knee and then left knee;

Slip either hand inside the opponent clinch, then apply another hand to control opponent lower head, then you can turn opponent to either side and knee strikes

Defenses against Teeb: block either Teeb with your palm or fore-arm [re-direct] to your outside left or right and follow up with leg kick;

Grab and re-direct left Teeb with your left hand, and counter with the left hook to the body and left knee

Grab and re-direct right Teeb with your right hand, and counter with a right punch to the body and right knee strike.

Level (3) Advance Muaythai Exam Techniques

Left Jab, left Teeb, right kick, clinch, right and left knees to strike
Jab, cross, right Teeb, left kick, clinch, right and left knee strike

Right straight punch, left hook, right knee, right elbow, push the opponent with a right hand, and left kick
Long jab, left hook, right punch, left knee, left and right elbow, push the opponent with a left hand, and right kick

Long jab, short jab, right kick, block the right punch, lock opponent right arm, grab the neck, pivot to your left, and right knee strike
Jab, cross, left kick, block left hook, lock opponent left arm, pivot to your right, and left knee strike

Unlock opponent clinch, grab neck with the right hand, lift his right arm, pivot, and sweep his front leg with your right foot
Unlock opponent clinch, grab neck with your left hand, lift his left arm, pivot and sweep his lead leg with your left foot

Jab, right kick, and right Teeb
Jab, cross, left kick and left Teeb
Jab, cross jab, right low, left kick to the body, and right kick to head
Grab opponent right leg kick, pull to your right, counter with a right kick to the body
Block opponent left kick with the left knee, left foot Teeb, and right back kick to the opponent body
Left Teeb, right Kick, right punch, left hook, clinch opponent neck, two Tee, and two Tang
Footwork around the ring for 3 minutes, move backward and throw left kick three times, move forward and throw right kick three times

Part IV

Proven fighting/winning Strategy for Fighters

Muaythai Vocabulary I for fighters

Mat = punch, Tae = Kick, TAAE = Jab, Trong = Straight punch, Vieng = Hook, Soi down = Uppercut, Sai = left, Kua = Right,

Muaythai Vocabulary II for fighters

Tae Vieng = Roundhouse Kick,

Tae tat = Cut kick,

Tae vieng krab = Back kick or spin back kick,

Tae lum Toi = Body kick,

Tae ka = Leg Kick,

Tae Soong = High kick,

Tae tum = Low kick,

Tae ket na = Straight Axe kick,

Teeb = Foot jab or push kick,

Teeb ka = Leg Teeb,

Teeb Na = Teeb to the face or Batha Loob Pak,

Sok = Elbow,

Kao = Knee,

Kao Loi = knee strike without the clinch,

kao Hol = knee strike with the clinch,

Sok Tat = Lead elbow,

Sok Trong = Rear elbow,

Sok Ngat = Up elbow,

Sok Nam = Down elbow

Mat = Punch,

Tae = Kick,

TAAE = Jab,

Trong = Straight punch,

Vieng = Hook,

Soi down = Uppercut,

Sai = Left,

Kua = Right

Muaythai Vocabulary III for fighters

Tat mala = (Block)Hand up with elbow cover your face and head

Hearn Vae Ha = Flying kick or knee

Ha noo mane hak el = Lock the waist and break the back

Thi na + Grab the foot or leg, raise them up and push forward

Sok Krab + back elbow

Pha Nga = Back off or lean backward

Thoi sark = Back off

Bata Loob Pak = Foot jab to the face

Jor ra kae phat ngang Spin back kick

Muaythai Foot Movement

Walk slightly and lightly on the ball of your feet

Move your right foot one step forward and to the right, then move your left foot following your right foot

Move your left foot one step forward and to your left, then move your right foot following your left foot

Do the same for moving forward and backward

Ranges of Muaythai Fight

Distance Fight = Use Teeb and Tae

Mid-Range Fight = Use Mat

Closed-Range Fight = Use Kao and Sok

Rhythm Techniques & Tactics for Muaythai Fight

Strike your opponent first before he strikes you

When you figure out how your opponent fight, you can wait for him to attack first, and then counter

If you figure out that you have a better chance, you can attack your opponent at the same time he attacks you

You should follow up your attack when you see your opponent is at disadvantages

Muaythai Proverb:

Push when being pulled, and

Pull when being pushed

Defense against Teeb

Move back

Step aside, left or right

Use your left hand to de-direct to the left, and follow up with rear foot kick

Confront by grabbing the foot with your hand, push forward and follow up with a kick

if your Teeb is grabbed by your opponent, break loose and Teeb again to get out

Tae

1. Tae Vieng = round house kick
2. Tae tat = cut kick
3. Tae tat Lang = cut kick low
4. Tae Sorn = kick the standing leg
5. Tae Vieng krab = spin or back kick (Jor Ra Kae fat nhang)

Defense against Tae Vieng

1. Thoi Sark = move back
2. Block by raising up your knee and elbow to block
3. Tae Sorn = kick the standing leg of your opponent when he uses the other leg to kick you
4. Step back to your left or right

5. Duck down if the opponent's kick is high
6. Move in fast and exchange with either lead or rear punch
7. Teeb your opponent's body or thigh

Move back to your right or left

Moving your right foot back to your right, followed by the left foot

Move your left foot back to your left, followed by the right foot

Tae-Tat & Defense against it

- Use your shin spiking down to the front of your opponent thigh, low leg, or sweep
- Defense against Tae tat:
- Move in close to your opponent and exchange with either lead or rear punch
- Step to your right, grab the kick with your left hand and throw a reverse punch
- Move in close with both hands up and one knee slightly up, and step in and push your opponent with your hands
- Step backward to the left or right
- Exchange and counter with a punch by letting your opponent's kick slightly hits you, but tighten your body's target area before the impact

Tae Tat Lang & Defense against it

- Sweep or kick low to the opponent's inside or outside leg
- To defend against it: Slightly raise your knee to block
- Teeb with your lead foot to your opponent's body or thigh
- Switch stand and move back

Tae Sorn

Tae Sorn

- Kick the standing leg
- If your opponent uses his lead leg to kick your lead leg, switch the stand
- If he uses his rear leg to kick, use your lead leg to kick his standing leg

- If your opponent uses his rear leg to kick your lead leg, move your lead parallel to your rear leg, after he misses the target, then use your rear leg to kick his standing leg

Tae Trong & Defense against it

- Kick straight up to the chest, or chin area of your opponent
- To defend against it, move back
- Move away by switching leg away

Tae Vieng Krab & Defense against it

Move back,

Teeb opponent leg,

move back, after your opponent misses, then kick his back area,

Raise your hands and Knee to block in close distance, or

push him away after block the kick, and follow up your technique

Defense against kicks/Conclusion

- Defense against low kick:
- Press your weight on foot, turning your shin against the incoming kick
- Move your lead foot back and use your rear foot to counter
- Teeb opponent's body or leg

Defense against Tae Lum Thoi

- Move back or lean back
- Block by raising up your knee
- Teeb opponent's leg or body

Defense against Tae Soong

- Lean back = Thoi sark

- Raising up knee, and counter
- Kick the standing leg (Tae Sorn or Tae Tat)
- Teeb opponent's body or leg

Mat Taae & Defense against it

Bang, Taae, Trong Vieng

Bang, step forward to your left, Vieng sai, Trong, Vieng sai

Move to your right, counter with Trong, Taae, Sok Kua

Move to your right, Ngat Kua, Vieng sai, Trong

Mat Trong & Defense against it

- Jab with lead hand or rear hand
- Tamala
- Teeb opponent body or leg
- Mat vieng or Mat trong
- Step Aside, and Mat Vieng Kao or Mat strong
- Thoi sark, and tae sai or kao
- Duck in or out and counter with mat vieng sai
- De-direct the mat, and counter with Tae, Kao, Sok or Mat

Defense against Kao Hol

- Use your Sok to block incoming kao
- Use mat Soi down to punch opponent abdomen
- Stay closed, and twist your body
- Bang with your kao or tat the incoming kao
- Unlock the Clinch, and Tee Sok
- Ha nu Mane hak el, place your foot behind the back of his foot, throw him back or to the side
- Grab his neck and swing his body in the same direction as his blow

Kao Ra

Kao Ra is a half kick and half knee. You strike your knee to your opponent when you are not too far or too close to him without Grabbing

Defense against Kao Ra

- Both elbow up and either knee up to block
- Move back
- Move in close and punch to the face or chest area
- Step aside and Re-direct the incoming knee and follow up with a punch

Kao tat = (When both fighters are wrestling, use either knee to spike opponent's ribs or legs)

- To defend, when opponent strike with his right knee, hold him tight and swing him to your right
- When he strikes with his left knee, swing him off balance to your left
- Grab his waist tight, press your chin and face to his upper chest, bear hug his lower back, and push him down

Kao Loi = (Jumping or flying knee, spiking to opponent face, chest, or abdomen)

- To defend, Step aside, use your hand to push him away, and follow up with a kick
- If he strikes with a right knee, move to your right, and counter with a right punch
- If he strikes with a left, move to your left, push him with your right hand, and punch him with a left hook
- Step aside, Teeb, kick, or punch, left or right

Mat Vieng & defense against it

- Pha Nga and Tae or Mat trong
- Bang with Tatmala and counter with Mat Vieng or trong
- Duck in or out and counter with Mat Vieng left or right

Sok & defense against it

(One hand up to cover your face, and throw your Sok to opponent face or mouth area)

- To defend, Pha Nga or move back
- In a close distance, Bang with Tatmala, and counter with your elbow
- There are: Tee Sok = use rear elbow, Sok tat = use lead elbow, Sok Ngat = up elbow
- To defend against Sok ngat, move back and counter with mat vieng
- Sok Krab = back elbow, and defend against it, Thoi and Teeb or Tae

Samples of Offensive Techniques:

- Tae sai, trong
- Tae Sorn, Teeb
- Tae kao, trong
- Teeb sai, Tae kao
- Teeb sai, kao sai
- Thoi Sark, Tae sai
- Pha Nga, Tae kao

Continued Offensive Techniques

- Taae, Trong, Tae Sai
- Pha Nga, move to your right, use your Rear Foot to Tae Kao
- Rear Foot Tae Lang, Same foot Teeb, Kao Loi sai
- Mat sai & kao, Teeb Sai
- Taae, taae, Teeb sai, Tae kao
- Taae, trong, Tae Sai, Tae kao

Continued Tech

- Taae, trong, kao Hol Sai & Kao Hol Kao
- Taae, trong, Kao sai
- Taae, Teeb sai, Tae Lang, Sok Krab, Kao sai

- Taae, Teeb, Tae Lang, Tae sai Soong
- Taae, Trong, Tae sai, Jor ra kae pat nhang
- Taae, trong, Sok sai, Kao Ra kao

Advices of How to Fight Different Size Opponent

- Tall opponent, make him come to you, stay in close distance, remain closed distance if successful, otherwise, move out fast
- Rusher, give opponent no room, move in and out, attack from outside
- Jabber, you need to fight in closed range, Block the jab, duck in and out, counter with body punch, kick inside and outside of opponent
- Slugger, keep moving, do not him get set, keep bothering him with inside and outside sudden attack, and move out quickly
- Southpaws make opponent come to you, circle to your left and prepare your right hand to block his left punch, use your right kick to attack his inside thigh and body, Use left hook often.

Part V Muaythai Clinches & Defenses

Clinches & Break the Clinches

Set 1

Lock upper neck and head, pull down/backward & Kao Hol

Grab the opponent head with right hand, lock his arm with your left arm, twist and pull with right arm on circular movement

When the opponent strikes with his right knee, use your left knee to strike inside his thigh of the standing leg, and right hand to pull, left hand to push, twist to your right side

Set 2

When your opponent clinches you, raise up your shoulder, and press opponent arm inward, use your right arm to grab his neck, and turn on circular movement to your right or left

When your opponent clinches you, grab his upper body and twist on circular movement

When the opponent clinches you, push his arm over your head, use your right arm to press his arm down, turn his head to your right, and Tee

When the opponent clinches you, slip one of your arms between his arms to control his neck and Tee

Set 3

When the opponent clinches you, use one hand to grab the opponent head, and another hand to push his armpit and turn in the circular movement

Raise up your knee to block the incoming knee and push

Raise up your knee under the opponent knee and turn the opponent in the circular movement

Raise up knee to block the incoming knee, a left hand holding his right arm, use your right hand to control his neck and Tee or Tank

When the opponent clinches your torso, garb his neck and upper shoulder, turn in to either side in a circular movement

Set 4

When the opponent clinches you, lock his waist, lift and throw

Lock under opponent arms and throw

Block the opponent right uppercut and control the opponent's opposite head and Tee

Block the punch and pull head down to the side and Tee

When countering the opponent's clinch, move one of your legs inside his and twist in a circular movement

Push the opponent left arm over your head, lock arms and control his head and Tee

Set 5

When the opponent rushing in to tackle you, you must jump around on his back and push him down

When you can't get out from the clinch, holding opponent tight, and do kao tat to the opponent's rib or thigh

When the opponent strikes, use your opposite kao to block or strike his inside thigh

When opponent clinch and pull you down, use one hand to pull down his arm, and another hand to lift his arm up in the reverse way and turn him down on his back

Use your foot to stop incoming kao, break the clinch and turn him over down on his back

Set 6

When opponent clinch you, lock his waist, lift and throw

Lock under opponent arms and throw

Block opponent right uppercut and control opponent's opposite head and Tee

Block the punch and pull head down to the side and Tee

When counter opponent clinch, move one of your leg inside his and twist in circular movement

Push opponent left arm over your head, lock arms and control his head and Tee

Conclusion

The Manual should conclude that Muaythai Techniques are suitable for both men and women to practice and hope the readers like the book and practice every technique they can. The book is not complete yet, and the writer will add more methods and some Muaythai articles that many Western Writers who had seen it and wrote about it in it later.

Nonetheless, the author hopes the readers understand where Muaythai comes from and how it is evolving through the history of Siam, Lanna, Lanxang, and other foreign countries that involved in the affairs of Siamese history such as Burma, Malaysia, France, Britain, Portugal, and Holland. The main reason that Siam changed its name to Thailand because its population is from Tai Kadai: (Thai-Lao, Thai-Lanna, Thai Malay, Thai-Khmer, and Thai-Mon). Siam represents only Sukhothai, Ayutthaya, Thonburi, and Krungthep (Bangkok). Therefore, the name "Thailand" represents its people. Thai Siamese is adventurists and wants to explore and conquer. For instance, Siam invaded Angkor Wat kingdom in 1549, but was defeated, and has tried again and again several times in the past, and even in the modern time, but was conquered by the Khmer and French Armies, or by the UN resolution. Some people speak Khmer in three provinces in Thailand: Buriram, Surin, and Sisaket. Buakaw Banchamek (Sombat Banchamek), A top Muaythai fighter, was born and grew up in Surin where half of the city, people speak Khmer, and the other half, speak Lao/ Lao Isan. People in five southern provinces in Thailand also speak Malay: Narathiwat, Pattani, Yala, Songkhla, Satun, some population in Ranong and Phuket also speak Malay. If the readers study Thailand neighbor countries' history, they would know that Siam had fought many wars against its neighbors and seized many territories (Thawin, 1977)

The rest of the pages are some pictures that the author gathered for **www.metayomuaythaica.com**, and an article title, which was written by Hardy Stockmann: **"Muaythai VS the Rest",** which was complimentary for Muaythai Academy of America Association where the author was training to be a Kru in 1991. The article proved that Muaythai is a proven ring competition, effective street self-defense, and top physical conditioning.

Muaythai

The Art of Siamese Un-armed Combat
By
Hardy Stockmana

Muay-Thai vs The Rest

The author can not provide the rest of article, but the readers can look it up and will understand better what its author wants them to know how effective Muaythai is against the rest of the world martial arts and maintains its superiority.

References

Khambou, P (1989) Forgetten Battle in Laos: Lao Resistant Force agianst Lao Communist Government. Wat Phu Archives, Champasak, Laos

Le Boise, P (1970) Qui est Laotian avec Fa-Ngum?: Et qui est-il? Lycee de Vientiane, Vientiane, Laos

Pavi, A (1966) Laos et La Histoire: Libraire National de Laos, Vientiane, Laos

Richardson, B (2014) English Used in Thai: An Incomplete Language? Fresno Print Shop Inc, Fresno, California

Sasombat, A (1990) Laos and its Battle with the Neighbors, United Printing Inc. Portland, Oregon

Sor Sae Lee (1982) The War between Laos and Vietnam: Revision of Lao History. United Printing Inc, Portland, Oregon

Stockmann, Hardy (1991) Top: Exalting in victory. a common sight in bouts between Muay-Thai and "other' • boxers.

Surichia, S (1976) Khmer Land & Thailand: The Seizure of Other Properties. Kao Publication Inc. Ubon, Thailand

Thawin, S (1977) Thailand: The Land of all Thais. Electric Printing Inc. Nakornphanom, Thailand

Hardy Stockman (1991) Muaythai Vs The Rest

www.ingramcontent.com/pod-product-compliance
Ingram Content Group UK Ltd.
Pitfield, Milton Keynes, MK11 3LW, UK
UKHW041833200726
13854UKWH00003BA/1112

9 780359 779024